Love Like Jesus

by

Katherine Ranga

Illustration

by

Patrick A. Malalo-an

Inspiring Ministries

Copyright © 2020 Katherine Ranga

All rights reserved. No part of this publication may be reproduced, distributed, or transmitted in any form or by any means, including photocopying, recording, or other electronic or mechanical methods, without the prior written permission of the publisher, except in the case of brief quotations embodied in critical reviews and certain other noncommercial uses permitted by copyright law. For permission requests, write to the publisher, addressed "Attention: Permissions Coordinator," at the address below.

ISBN: 978-1-64871-933-2 (Electronic)
ISBN: 978-1-64871-949-3 (Paperback)

Front cover image by Patrick Malalo-an

First printing edition 2020.

Inspiring Ministries
Any enquiries are to be directed to Inspiring Ministries and the below e-mail address.
beinspired2read@gmail.com

www.inspiringministries.net.au

Love Like Jesus

Inspiring Ministries

The love of Jesus is like no other.

He loves ALL people just like
a sister or brother.

He sees no colour, creed or race.
He sees the heart and not the face.

He came to earth to teach us how,
To love each other once again somehow.

In joy and peace and harmony.
This is His dream for us, you see.

So when you're out at play together,
LOVE like Jesus and share forever...

Your toys, smiles, and your laughter too...
With someone new, who's not like you.

And you will see a better place.
At home, at school, and in your crèche.

A place that's rich and full of colour,
With beautiful people all different from each other.

It takes both you and I,
great and small, to love like Jesus.
Then Jesus will smile down at you because
He sees your heart is true.
AND...

Because he loves you too!

Glossary to Difficult Concepts or Words

Creed - The religion a person believes in, or a set of rules they follow.

Race - It is how we group each other based on our physical or social differences. For example, some people from a race may have light skin, while from another race they may have dark skin.

Harmony - When we are happy together or something works well with something else.

Creche - Where small children go to learn or school for little children.

Bio

Katherine Ranga was born in New Zealand and now resides in Perth, Western Australia. Her first experience with God was as a child, which inspired her to write her first book Jesus Loves Me. What followed was the Christian Learning Book series, designed to guide children into a personal relationship with God and Jesus.

Other books written by Katherine Ranga are, Jesus Loves Me, Love Like Jesus, We Three The Trinity, First Love – God Stories, Ollie and the Mouse, Oscar wants to Come Too and Ollie's Garden.

Alon Makes a Difference; also written by Katherine Ranga as a collaborative works with Brian Williams. Katherine and Brian wanted to inspire and empower the children to make a difference by taking control of waste in their environments and communities.

Made in the USA
Monee, IL
04 May 2026